Hustling For Cash Money With Metal Recycling!!!

By

Domenic Costa

dcosta1smallhaul@gmail.com

Now let's go make some money!!!!

INTRODUCTION

I earn an extra $100-150.00+ per month

without any super human effort, money, or fuel "Hustling For Cash Money With Metal Recycling!" It's true and I do! This book will teach you about our most recycled metals and plastics that are recycled for cash! You can hustle for cash money with metal recycling and it is easy! When you change how you look at the world, it is amazing how things that were invisible to you once before will suddenly appear right before your eyes! This thought process of thinking about what you want to see and then seeing it will change your life!!!! Every time I see an abandoned refrigerator on my drive home I see a $10 bill US (at the current rate of 4 to 8 cents per pound). I see more recyclables ($s) than I ever did before!

Here's what you're going to learn:

Chapter 1: The Four Why's
Chapter 2: Time For Double D's (Not Those, But Due Diligence!)
Chapter 3: What Are Your Goals?
Chapter 4: What Do You Need?
Chapter 5: Getting Set Up!
Chapter 6: Breaking Down Items-Time In Versus Profitability
Chapter 7: Collect!
Chapter 8: Network Baby!
Chapter 9: Collect More and Make More!!!

CHAPTER 1
The Four Why's

Why #1?

To make extra money! Money isn't everything but it sure can help you survive or improve your lot/lifestyle! This income stream will add to your budget! These streams of income along with any other money/job/hustle you have will increase your daily/monthly/annual cash income flow. This recycling hustle can be a budget difference maker for your life and relieve some of your budget stress. Also, there is the intrinsic value of making where you live a little bit cleaner, safer, and better to look at! You can drive or walk around where you live and see less trash because it's getting picked up and recycled. A better environment where our air, soil, and water can be better for everyone where we live and put some money in our pockets, too! It is a win/win situation!

Why #2

It is psychologically satisfying to make cash money by yourself and for yourself with NO BOSS! You are in charge! How much effort you expend is up to you. Many of my brother and sister recyclers/scrappers drive around either the night before or the early morning of trash pick-up days to find trash-to-cash recycling treasures. I currently do not but by keeping my eyes open during my commute to and from work I generate $100-150.00+ per month cash!

Why #3

It is physically satisfying! Getting active and using your body in a physical way to do all this helps your body get in shape and helps release feel-good endorphins!!!! As the wise man said, "Today is the youngest you're ever going to be." That's true! Let's get our bodies moving and our minds engaged! Staying active with recycling can help you maintain fitness levels to enjoy your non-work activities even more!

Why #4

It is spiritually satisfying! Remove stuff that can environmentally and visually pollute where you live!! Get a sense of giving back to the world you were born into and leave it better!!! It is very rewarding to make your living, work, drive, and walk through areas of your life more appealing because there will be less junk and trash to view because you hustled and made a difference while putting some money in your pocket. This recycling is like doing your good deed for the day and you get paid! That's crazy good! If you believe in Karma that's even better energy you are creating for the universe by doing good works! That's a win-win situation if there ever was one. Cash money is a great motivator!

Chapter 2
Time for Double D's (Not Those but Due Diligence!!!!)

Due Diligence for this chapter is finding out what can be recycled where you live, who is paying for those recyclables, how much are they paying for those items, where are they located, what is their distance from you (transportation costs), and what are their days and hours of operation?

What are we collecting?: Here are some examples:

-Plastic drink containers
-Glass drink containers
-Aluminum can drink containers
-Copper (pipe, stripped wire, #1, #2)
-Aluminum cast, clean, and dirty
-Aluminum wire
-Aluminum sheet (painted and clean)
-Brass
-Magnets
-Lead
-Solid/Cast/Wrought Iron
-Pressed Steel/Tin like: File cabinets, refrigerators, freezers, etc...)
-Mixed Metal: Power and Garden Tools, small home appliances (microwaves, toasters, vacuum cleaners, etc...)

What countries do this besides the USA? (This is a partial listing of countries where this may be possible and if not then it should be!):
-Canada
-Great Britain

-Ireland
-South Africa
-Italy
-France
-Spain
-Germany
-Romania
-China
-Japan
-South Korea
-Vietnam
-Australia
-New Zealand
-Lebanon
-India
-Iraq
-Turkey
-Greece
-Portugal

Do you have recyclers that pay cash money close to you (close being determined by you if what is described in this book is even possible to do where you live!!!)?
Find out where the recyclers are and their hours of operation as well as what days they are open. Some countries or states may not have mandatory recycling for drink containers but may have paying recyclers for metals. Find out what is possible and returnable for cash in your location. If you are fortunate enough to have many recyclers, this can be a big bonus. You will be able to compare prices ($), hours of operation, days of the week open, customer care/service, and proximity to you that best suits your personal situation. This step is crucial yet illuminating to initiating your recycling journey for *cha-ching* cash money!!! Due Diligence (Double D's) will answer your questions to guide your decisions on the

possibilities of "Hustling For Cash Money With Metal Recycling!!!"

Chapter 3
What Are Your Goals?

This is huge for ALL life undertakings in my estimation! Goal setting makes things in your life a possibility! Sitting and thinking on this gets your mind ready, which is the spark for your physical actions! Try listening to Earl Nightingale's "The Strangest Secret" on YouTube! His spoken words will and can be a source of life-changing motivation to ANY goal you have in life. You WILL learn as you go on your recycling journey and keep yourself aware and ready to grow and improve your processes! Your goals may include how much you wish to make full or part time by the day, week, month, or year. What abilities do you have to undertake this like your health, physical capabilities, storage space, transportation, family commitments, work responsibilities, etc..... What will you do with your money after you make your stacks of cash?

My goals always included the Triple FFF's. They are Financial, Family, and Fun. It is such a feeling of accomplishment to add to a bank account, add to a retirement account, add to an emergency fund, or pay down a mortgage or two! It was also rewarding to treat my family to a special meal or contribute to a vacation fund for a bigger vacation. Fixing a toy or one of my hobby/fun items was personally rewarding as well. Doing all of these things without touching the regular family budget dollars was fun! The Triple FFF's (Financial, Family, and Fun) goals motivate me! Spend a little time thinking about what motivates you! Set some goals with some steps and get after it! Achieving goals can get some satisfaction flowing in your life and the memories of achieving them build your self-esteem and will energize and propel you through the hard times, which most certainly occur. Building your self-esteem and increasing your knowledge of delayed gratification AKA, "The Really Good Stuff", comes after you work hard and smart. This can sustain your mental, physical, and spiritual energies and get you to some goals being achieved! This is truly a positive beast that will feed itself and help you live a GREAT life! Now go get it done!!!

Chapter 4
What do you need?

How do you transport yourself where you live? Is it by foot, bicycle, motorcycle, car, or truck? Are you going to put your stuff that you collect in plastic bags, cardboard boxes, trashcans, or bins? Where are you going to keep it once you have it? To make it worth your efforts you need to store usually great amounts (depends what you are collecting) to generate lots of cash when you finally bring it in to your favorite or closest recycling/redemption center! Storage can be done with smaller areas too-- especially if you are collecting the pricier metals! Small autos can get the job done as well as small to medium to full-size trucks. Obviously a big truck though, can handle bigger and odd size pieces/items/appliances.

The value of your time is up to you of course! You need to figure out at a minimum of what your energy or fuel costs will be. Driving 20 miles with your bike to earn 3 bucks over 3 hours is better than nothing if your back is against the wall! But doing that in any gas/diesel vehicle is not business smart! Let's face it kids, our best asset we get as humans is our time!!! Respecting your time and using it well will better your life and put some cheddar (cash) in your pockets!!!

In my situation I load a full size (8 foot bed) truck in about 15 minutes, drive to my recycling center and unload to get the cash in an additional 20 minutes, before heading home for a final 15 minutes. This is a round trip of about 1 hour where I will clear after fuel costs about $20 dollars US. $20 bucks an hour works for me!!! Your situation very well maybe different but this is the current acceptable minimum I will accept! You need to have this conversation with yourself so you can make the best decisions!

Do you have family members, friends, or a partner(s) to work with? Including someone can help a lot in this labor-intensive business but it can also create opportunities for quality time as well. If you are a parent, what better way to model a work ethic for a child than to bring them with you as you hustle for cash money with metal recycling! The time shared with my own kids has been priceless. Back when I recycled newsprint (old newspapers), my two kids, when the help wasn't looking, would climb the majestic paper peaks of paper and slide down them! It's urban sledding, ghetto-style I know, but they had a ton of fun! The locations, situations, and people we've seen have been alternatingly wonderful, appalling, and hilarious! Sometimes all three have appeared with one incident with some great-observed life lessons throughout each one. It helped teach to look for opportunity and seize it when it appears. Now that's a life lesson a parent can impart to their children and feel good about! Remember they are watching what we do with a whole lot more weight than what we say as parents. Get out there and lead/show them with our positive actions! Remember to have extra gloves and remind them to dress appropriately for the day's job. This would include closed toe shoes, clothes that can get dirty, long sleeve shirts, and long pants. Really young children probably need to stay in your vehicle or near your side at ALL times! Safety first!

Chapter 5
Getting Set Up!

I highly recommend having some space where you can store your collectibles so you can collect enough to make it worth your efforts when you turn them in. Side and backyards are perfect. Garages can do the job, too. If you are a tenant you will know what is acceptable and where it will be allowed to be able to store your stuff. Some metals, like the different kinds of iron, come in different shapes and can eat up your space as you accumulate it so you will need space or you will have to limit the types of items you collect.

Large 33 or more gallon plastic bags you can seal or tie up to close are perfect for many redemptive items like aluminum or plastic drink containers and you diminish or eliminate any vermin (insects, mice, etc....) problems. I use those bags inside of old trashcans with lids and as the cans/bags fill up I can pull them out for placement in my storage area. A new bag goes in to my trashcan and a new collection begins.

I keep three 33-gallon trashcans to separate my family's glass drink containers into their respective colors of green, amber/brown, and clear. This saves a bit of time and getting my hands dirty when I bring them in for cash. Many redemptive centers require that glass be separated into their respective colors in order to get paid. I drive these same glass-filled trashcans to the recycling/redemptive centers and move my already separated glass into the center's containers/trashcans to save time and keep clean.

I currently use about four 5 gallon buckets in my outdoor storage area to separate out some pricier metals. I put smaller copper bits and pieces I come across in one. I put brass in another. I keep 2 buckets for all the copper wire I come across from appliances. I drill nice sized 1/8 to 1/4 inch holes in the bottom of the buckets for water/rain drainage and of course small kid and pet safety.

Gloves are a must to keep clean from the collected containers (aluminum, glass, and plastic drink containers typically) and to protect your fingers/hands from injury when handling especially heavy, sharp metallic objects or broken glass. I use cheap vinyl gloves especially for when I'm turning in my drink containers. They often have residual drink fluids in them and can get a bit nasty to handle when you turn them in. When you bring them in for cash you usually have to empty them from your bags to the recycling center's containers. Getting these juices on your hands can suck!!!! I use cheap heavier leather gloves for the handling of my bulkier, heavier, and often sharp edged metallic collectibles. Bleeding cuts suck! Smashed fingers are no fun! Keep a couple of pairs in your vehicle! You will appreciate them as you slide that abandoned refrigerator into the back of your truck or move that greasy old stove or BBQ as well.

Please wear shoes! Broken glass and bare feet don't mix! Dropping heavy stuff on your toes doesn't end well typically either! One emergency room visit in this day and age can wipe out multi years of profits!!! Be safe kids!!!

I keep a couple of magnets in the back of my truck bed to ascertain if some items I come across are iron-based metals. Some recycling centers collect magnets for cash but I kept a couple of big speaker magnets for this job. You may have a Harbor Freight Tools store in your local region (http://www.harborfreight.com/) and have magnets too for the low-low price!

Some basic tools are a must. A small pair of wire clip/cutters is perfect for removing copper filled appliance wires/cords. One each of a Phillips screwdriver as well as a standard flat head screwdriver are great for opening, removing, or prying off anything metallic you come across. A small sledge hammer (1lb) is useful for breaking apart or down BBQs that I find too. As an upgrade, a rechargeable variable speed drill with various size and types of bits (flathead, Phillips, Torx, hex, etc...) will save the muscles in your forearms and decrease the amount of time you take apart or breakdown any item! As you know, whenever you get more efficient with your time, you increase your profitability!

Keeping a container of low cost wipes in your vehicle or storage area is great for cleaning up anything that spills. They are great for cleaning your hands as well. Paper towels, bottled water, snacks, and anything else that you can think of to make your collection journey clean and comfortable is also great to keep on hand! Proper and regular hydration can keep you hustling and out of the hospital or worse!

Chapter 6
Breaking Down Items-- Time In Versus Profitability

This chapter will come down to you and your thoughts and personal money situation. If I'm pressed for time maybe I don't breakdown that cast aluminum and pressed steel BBQ and just dump it with the rest of my general metal load. Truthfully for me, 99% of the time I'll take apart those cast aluminum BBQs because I know if I accumulate a couple of those dirty cast aluminum BBQ cases I'll have at a minimum a $35-$40 cash score for 15 minutes of personal labor from me! That's $140-$160 per hour! Help your planet; help your local ecology, and your wallet too!!!! Higher end models of BBQ/Grillers also have brass (copper and zinc alloy) burners, which also have a great return! Simply scratch the burners with a tool/nail and if it reveals a bright yellow color then you have scored! (8 cents per pound for iron versus $1.65 per pound for brass!)* These were the prices at the time of this writing and are based on my location in Southern California, the Los Angeles Harbor area.

Some people will strip electrical wires and appliance cords to reveal the pricey copper metal versus the lower price per pound of dirty copper cord. This can be time intensive and it has not worked out for me time versus cash or ROI (Return On Investment). Your situation may vary and it may work for you. There are YouTube videos available with different ideas on how to construct one as well. It may be worth it to strip your wires because stripped power cords become #1 copper and can quadruple your price per pound! Again you've got to personally measure your time and how much cord you have.

On another note, your power cords may have brass male parts, which slide into wall outlets. A simple twist with a pair of pliers will pop them out in seconds and you can save them in your brass storage bucket. Again, this is all about your own personal decision on your use of time.

Chapter 7
Collect!

You're all set up and ready to collect! I start at home! My locale charges a redemption fee for each drink container in plastic, glass, or aluminum that my family purchased at any type of store. Why put your paid redemptive fees into your city's weekly recycle bin when you can keep it yourself? Start with those, bag 'em, and when you reach what you believe is a large enough amount for your vehicle, get them in and get your money!

As you do any of your regular driving from your home, keep your eyes open for any recyclables and scoop them up! A lot of great stuff is left curbside in both residential and multi-unit neighborhoods especially the night before or the morning of regularly scheduled trash pick up days. Try to "own" your own neighborhood for big appliance recyclables. Sometimes a good time to keep your eyes open and head on a swivel is on the weekends. Many do-it-your-selfers complete their tasks on the weekends and place their old metal stuff/large appliances out anytime from Saturday afternoon through Sunday night. If you see something in a driveway and if you have time, stop and knock on the door. Ask to take it and offer to help by taking any other recyclables away. If they're not home, try leaving a handwritten note on one of your new business cards with your request. I got a lot of stuff this way and got future regular customers as well! If your drive is by commercial or manufacturing properties, you will see things as well. People will appreciate that you are helping them. Speak respectfully. Dress decently (look and be clean with no offensive slogans or pictures on t-shirts for example).

If you have a regular job, recyclables may be at your fingertips as well! Keep your eyes and ears open at your regular worksite. One Sunday at my most visited recycling center, I witnessed a group of 3 men bring a type of large (it fit into the back of a regular 8' truck bed) copper distiller from a job worksite that scored them a $3500+ cash score! Wow!!! One plumber friend kept his scrap copper and brass which he turns in once a year after the US's Thanksgiving holidays for usually $3000+ to fund his family's Christmas and New Year's holiday (gifts, foods, and parties)! Their holiday parties were outstanding!!!

As you've changed your mindset to that of a cash making recycler, you will be amazed at what you will begin to see! Getting your mind dialed in for ANY task is the 1st step for success! You'll see!!! Things you previously drove or walked by before and did not see will suddenly become apparent to you. Pick them up and profit! Changing your mindset or view of the world will change your life. As humans, the way we look at and perceive our world around us determines our quality and quantity of life. Spend a little time and ponder the information in this paragraph. You will change your life! Be prepared to be amazed!

If you have any of the brands of Smartphone's please consider adding a Craigslist app like Craigslist Pro where you can install a phone alert for specific recycling items where you live! If the alerts match your time capabilities, you will be able to respond to those curb alerts in your neighborhood for metals typically or anything else you are trying to find! People want to get rid of their items as soon as possible. When you respond to their Craigslist ads you are helping them. Don't forget to knock on the door, introduce yourself, and ask if they have any other recyclables you could remove for them. If they are not home, leave a card/note with your contact information. Oops, we are getting to Chapter 8's focus!

Chapter 8
Network Baby!

It's simple really! Let people know what you are doing. Own what you do. Let people know you can pick up their broken stuff for a low, low price or even free! Get cards made with your contact information I use Vistaprint for low cost and professional looking cards and here is the link:
http://www.vistaprint.com/vp/welcome.aspx?no_redirect=1&xnav=top
Pass them out wherever and whenever you're out. The human network will grow and the calls will come in! It takes time but it will spread how you are helping people solve a problem by removing their unwanted/broken stuff that they don't know how to get rid of or don't have the desire nor energy to get rid of or recycle it themselves. Leave your cards at every stop and your network will grow. Some folks will begin bringing you their recyclables and dropping them off where you live! Recyclables will be attracted to you! You have become a human magnet! Creating this network will increase your profits! Get out there and network! It pays off!!!

I have some videos on my YouTube channel "Coach Dom Costa" under the playlist: Hustling For Cash Money With Metal Recycling!!! Here' the link:
http://www.youtube.com/playlist?list=PLYPn0SqDBpCpVeyTftQCsvJgVmZ4rHo5u
You can see some of my hauls, storage techniques, scrap loads, what my network brings me, and of course pictures of the cash money I make and YOU can make too! Check it out, plus of course like, share, comment, and subscribe!

Chapter 9
Collect More and Make More!!!

The more you do this, the more it will become easier and the more efficient you'll become in all of your processes of collection, storage, and reclamation for cash! It's true! You'll be amazed! As time went by, I had more experiences that taught me, shaped me, and sharpened my scrapping/hustling/recycling skills. That's a great lesson for all of life's endeavors! Sometimes you just have to sit down, think, get an idea, and get started. We are all terminal on this planet (don't mean to get too heavy)! Get started on something and get busy living! Go make that money and have that fun!

Check out other recyclers/scrappers on YouTube besides me to gain knowledge of other recycling skills and tips. Just go to YouTube (http://www.youtube.com/) and type into the search box what you want to learn like metal recycling or scrapping and spend some time watching, listening, and learning. These video authors enlightened, entertained, and taught me a ton of skills that shortened my learning curve on the path of improving my efficiency and ultimately my profitability!

Chapter 10
Cash in your Recyclable Chips!

Your schedule is clear and your storage spaces are approaching full. It's time to load up what you have and bring it in to get that cash! Tie it down! Don't cause an accident or damage your vehicle! This is especially true with big appliances or odd metal shapes like bed frames, curtain rods, metal furniture, etc.... Always have if possible more than one place to bring your recyclables to. Comparing prices from your cash-paying recyclers for your collected items is your own due diligence (Double D's) to ensure the profits your hard work needs to receive the maximum cash you can for your efforts! A simple phone call or a mouse click is all it takes to put extra dollars in your pocket!

Enjoy the day you bring it in! You had a plan. You worked your plan. So now enjoy the fruits of your labor. You set goals for the money you're making. Put that money at those goals! Make progress on those goals and note it! Those good feelings you get today for your accomplishments are going to be your fuel for your next round of collections. Congratulations Hustler/Scrapper!!!

270021

Purch No.

6/2/2013   10:06:45AM
General Customer
Passengers: 0

Item COPPER #1(1)
Weight   2.0
Price   2.5500

Item PAINTED ALUM
Weight   86.0
Price   0.3000

Item YL BRASS (1)
Weight   13.0
Price   1.6500

Item COPPER #2(1)
Weight   7.0
Price   2.5000

Item INSU WIRE #2
Weight   20.0
Price   0.4000

Please Give To Cashier

Chapter 11
REPEAT!!!!

Here's a recap of our chapter titles! Once you are set up with your schemes, dreams, goals and mindset, you are ready to simply repeat the information of Chapters 7, 8, 9, and 10!

Chapter 7 Collect! (Get it, break it down, and store it!)

Chapter 8 Network Baby! (Talk it up! Offer your services!)

Chapter 9 Collect More and Make More!!! (See it, get it, break it down, and store it!)

Chapter 10 Cash In Your Recyclable Chips! (Get that money!)

Chapter 11 REPEAT!!!!

Chapter 12
How this All Started-Josephine's Story

The school year that this story takes place in, the majority of my students consisted of 9th graders in my Integrated Coordinated Science classes. My school mostly had kids from low to moderate/middle income families. 9th graders (14 to 15 years old) at a grade 9 through 12 school are very energetic as they go on the puberty conveyor belt to adolescence and adulthood and can be very immature at times as well. The majority are, for the most part, beautiful human beings who cannot control themselves that well yet.

Josephine was a member of my classes. She, like so many other of the students, had cell phones. This was at the time when iPhones had been around for about 2 years and were very popular with all of their abilities. Not everyone had one because they or their families could not afford one. Josephine was part of this group and had an older model flip phone. On this day, during the class group activities I was monitoring, she was bemoaning the fact that she could not get one of those phones because she was broke and being 14 she wasn't even old enough (Los Angeles, California) to even attempt to get a work permit to work at your typical minimum wage fast food institution or store. (You have to be 16 to get one!) This caught my attention because in my experience of being raised by a self-employed building contractor and his bookkeeping wife, you could make way more than minimum wage by hustling and providing a service for others. All of this could be done at ANY age without a work permit! I stopped the class and shared this "Biology of Life" story that I would challenge her "I can't afford it" mindset by showing how I would make money with NO or little money!

This is where the journey began for this book: "Hustling for Cash Money With Metal Recycling!!! I turned a $25 start-up investment to over 3k in about 12 months! I did this while sharing this journey with all of my classes. My moneymaking hustling activities consisted of a mix of storage auction resales, yard sales, Craigslist Free resales, small hustle/labor jobs, and of course, metal recycling! These were all done as examples for the kids. This "Biology of Life" story nearly always had a student or two in each class share their service or opportunistic story of their "hustling" escapades. Their money making endeavors ranged from babysitting, yard sales, washing/detailing cars, yard work, housecleaning, selling Christmas Lenox ornaments their Mom was going to throw away on EBay, helping senior citizens with chores, etc... Yes we did cover our "California State Standards for Science", but we also shared our "Biology of Life" of acquiring the mindset and vision to attempt to earn the money to get that better cell phone, provide for your needs, provide for your family, or help others. A big thank you goes to "Josephine" whose story has inspired many a conversation in many classes since that time to go out, see what you want, get off your butt, plan, act decisively, and get what you want in life! Life is a short ride with an end--get moving kids!!!

Chapter 13
The Hoarder House

Networking gave us this job of cleaning out the appliances out of a single-family home of an older woman who recently had been moved to an assisted-living facility. I had been called because her next-door neighbor, my friend, had been keeping an eye on the home and had access with keys. Her concern was the smell in the kitchen because the stuffed refrigerator was leaking for some reason in the kitchen and was literally rotting and sinking through the wood floor! It turns out that this appliance was stuffed with up to seven year old dated-rotting food! With my son's help, we cleared out all of the appliances in the home, threw out all of the rotting-old food, and closed the natural gas for this property as well to lower the chances for a house fire! This lady was not moving back according to my friend and her nearest relative was a niece who lived in Australia! My son got to see a real hoarder's house with 9 months of mail stacked on the kitchen table, hallways with so much stacked in them you had to walk sideways, dozens of fast-food Styrofoam drink cups stacked perfectly in the bathroom, to a washing machine so stuffed with bed sheets that a family of trapped mummified mice were in the bottom of the tub!!! We received over $200 from the woman's relative for removing the appliances plus we made over $100 in recycling all of the appliances and any metal we could find in the yard too! Pretty cool stuff and I got to share this experience with my son with pretty good conversations on depression and hoarding behavior! Just another day of HUSTLING!!!!

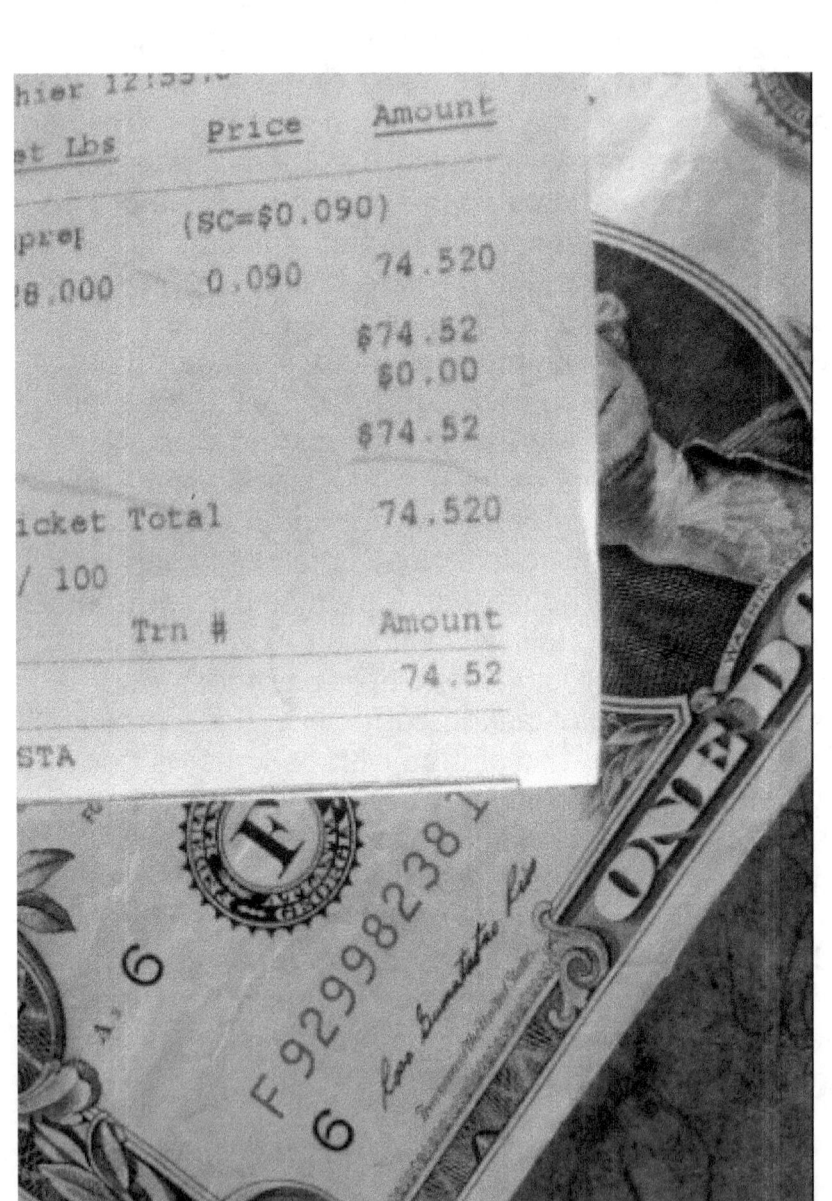

hier 12:55

et Lbs   Price   Amount

prep   (SC=$0.090)

8.000   0.090   74.520

                              $74.52
                              $0.00

                              $74.52

icket Total   74.520

/ 100

        Trn #   Amount

                              74.52

STA

Conclusion
Everyday Hustlin' For That Cash Money!!!!

I have a full time job and I have a full size truck. I have a 2 mile one way trip to work. I also use my truck for a "Small Haul" moving, estate-garage-storage unit-home-apartment clean out, side-hustle business! I am fortunate! I pick up a high percentage of my stuff just by going back and forth to work and perhaps taking the "long way home"-dipping through alleys, behind malls, businesses, and taking different streets to work and home. The Craigslist Pro app I have used with alerts on my iPhone for metals available close to me has been great when my schedule allows me to get them. As friends, some clients, and neighbors see what I'm doing, they will call me to pick up their recyclables for them (free of course or low cost)! This all adds to my cache of cash-making recyclable items! I used to worry in my past life what others thought of me or if they giggled or snickered at why a grown-ass professional is now the Sanford and Son of their world. I don't care and I love it!!!! I laugh as I keep stacking that cash and provide for my loved ones and achieve bit by bit my financial and life goals. The students in my classes dig the stories and YouTube videos. Their newfound "Hustles" inspire me as I've hoped I inspired them as well. In fact I have found that most of the people in my life are encouraging of my efforts and most importantly my family is cheering me on as I/we enjoy the fruits of my labor! Here's to you and your journey! Get recycling and make that money!! This life is a short ride!!!! Let's roll!!!!

Salute!
Best wishes and luck!
Domenic Costa

P.S.-I'd love your comments, reviews, and critiques! Leave them here or contact me at: dcosta1smallhaul@gmail.com. I have quite a few YouTube videos too on this book's topic that I know you'll find informative and helpful as well! I have a special playlist with lots of videos on my metal/scrapping/recycling adventures. They are informative and inspiring! (Well I like to think so! LOL!) Check them out!! (http://www.youtube.com/playlist?list=PLYPn0SqDBpCpVeyTftQCsvJgVmZ4rHo5u)

You can also find on Twitter:

https://twitter.com/CostaDomenic

I've been blessed and married to my beautiful bride for over 20+ years and I can/want any input to get better! Thank you so much and happy scrappin'!!!

Acknowledgements

A big, big thank you to my wife Pamela and my children, Lauren and Jacob, for all of your love, support, editing skills, and inspiration on Daddy's many adventures! I also want to thank Glendon Cameron for the Hustlin' and Creatin' inspiration (check him out on YouTube, Twitter, and Facebook). A BIG thank you to you for choosing this book and taking a chance on my recipe for success! This is my big thank you as well for reading this book all the way to the end. If you have liked what you have read please take a moment to leave a review for this book on Amazon:

https://www.amazon.com/review/create-review?ie=UTF8&asin=B00FF1VF1W&channel=detail-glance&nodeID=&ref_=dp_top_cm_cr_acr_wr_link

Disclaimer and FTC Notice

NOW GET OUT THERE AND HUSTLE!!!